Georgia Duncan
Illustrations by Adriana Ciołko

Before You Were Born

Bumblebee Books
London

BUMBLEBEE PAPERBACK EDITION

Copyright © Georgia Duncan 2022
Illustrations by Adriana Ciolko

The right of Georgia Duncan to be identified as author of this work has been asserted in accordance with sections 77 and 78 of the Copyright, Designs and Patents Act 1988.

All Rights Reserved

No reproduction, copy or transmission of this publication
may be made without written permission.
No paragraph of this publication may be reproduced,
copied or transmitted save with the written permission of the publisher, or in accordance with the provisions of the Copyright Act 1956 (as amended).

Any person who commits any unauthorised act in relation to
this publication may be liable to criminal
prosecution and civil claims for damage.

A CIP catalogue record for this title is
available from the British Library.

ISBN: 978-1-83934-661-3

Bumblebee Books is an imprint of
Olympia Publishers.

First Published in 2022

Bumblebee Books
Tallis House
2 Tallis Street
London
EC4Y 0AB

Printed in Great Britain

www.olympiapublishers.com

Dedication

I dedicate this book to the Lord Jesus Christ, the lover of my soul. And to my beautiful children, Calleigh and Harper, and my arrow in Heaven. Lastly to my best friend, encourager, intercessory prayer partner and love, Benjamin.

Sweet, sweet baby
Sent from above,
The way that the heavens
Pour out God's love.

Before you were born
He set you apart
And tucked you in close
To the Father's heart.

He **created** your being
In the secret place
And made every **expression**
On your precious face.

Psalm 139:15

He knit you together
Inside your mothers womb.

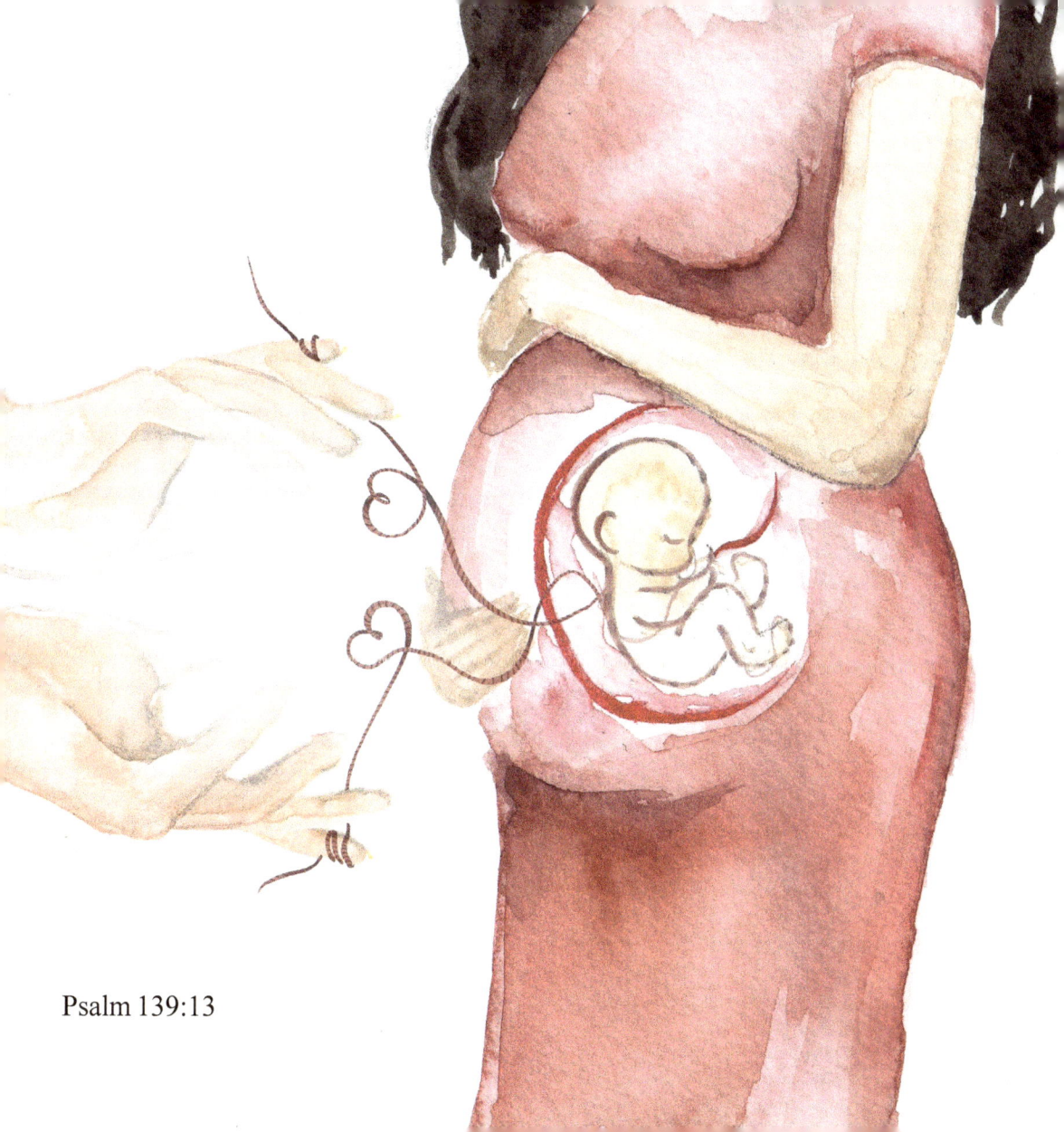

Be it never too late...

...and never too soon for God's **perfect** will to Always surround you.

2 Thessalonians 3:3

He knew every hair
That would mark your head
And **created** your tongue
To speak **life** to the dead.

Luke 12:7
Proverbs 18:21

He **prepared** in advance
The things you are **called** to do.

Ephesians 2:10

And sent Holy Spirit
To fill and guide you.

Acts 2:4

Your heritage is great
Wide and unseen.
Your heritage is that
Of a righteous King.

Psalm 127:3

And as you grow
My prayer for you
Is that you will see yourself
How Jesus sees you.

Luke 10:19

When life gets uncertain
And you feel far away,
Always remember this,
Prayer that I pray.

Deuteronomy 31:6

For a life of abundance
in this new world called home.

Never forgetting your true Father sits on the throne.

John 10:10

Jeremiah 1:5
"Before I formed you in the womb I knew you, before you were born I set you apart; I appointed you as a prophet to the nations"

Psalm 139:15
You even formed every bone in my body when you created me in the secret place; carefully and skillfully you shaped me from nothing to something.

Psalm 139:13
You created my inmost being; you knit me together in my mother's womb.

2 Thessalonians 3:3
But the Lord is faithful, and he will strengthen you and protect you from the evil one.

Luke 12:7
Indeed, the very hairs of your head are numbered. Don't be afraid, you are worth more than many sparrows.

Proverbs 18:21
The tongue has the power of life and death, and those who love it will eat its fruit.

Ephesians 2:10
For we are God's handiwork, created in Christ Jesus to do good works, which God prepared in advance for us to do.

Acts 2:4
All of them were filled with the Holy Spirit and began to speak in other tongues as the Spirit enabled them.

Psalm 127:3
Children are a heritage from the Lord, offspring a reward from Him.

Luke 10:19
I have given you the authority to trample on snakes and scorpions and to overcome the power of the enemy; nothing will harm you.

Deuteronomy 31:6
Be strong and courageous. Do not be afraid or terrified because of them, for the LORD your God goes with you; He will never leave you nor forsake you.

John 10:10
The thief comes to steal kill and destroy, but I have come that they may have life and have it more abundantly.

A Prayer For My Baby

_____

_____

_____

_____

_____

_____

_____

_____

About the Author

I am a sinner saved by grace! My testimony is that of death to life. If I had to sum up my life with a verse it would be Genesis 50:20 But you planned evil against me, but God meant it for good in order to bring about this present result, to save many people alive. The very reason I even write is to be sure and let everyone know, Jesus saves, Jesus loves you, and you were created with a purpose.

Lightning Source UK Ltd.
Milton Keynes UK
UKHW050611220223
417397UK00003B/49